QUOTES AND ACTIVATIONS

FOR LIFE EVERYDAY

Women who got out of their comfort zones

With

Apostle Alicia George

Introduction

These women birthed this book with me because we can all be queen friends. As these women lay out quotes and Activations to glean from it proves that as women, we do not have to always know each other personally to encourage each other.

As they become co-authors in a small project it opens doors for big things to happen. Throughout these pages are strong women who for the first time stepped out of their comfort zones to share so that whoever reads a quote and activation will know that they too are able to take a leap of faith.

Dedication

To Queen friends who always know that there is something to say but have not figured out how. Always know it just takes an idea, and know that there are other women queen friends waiting to support you.

Do not despise small beginnings.

Apostle Alicia George

Apostle Alicia George is also known as a crystal clear Vision Coach, certified in Business, Branding and Speaking she is the founder of Boss Business Coaching. LLC. Her first love is God and Ministry.

Quote

To Live is the rarest thing in the world.

Most people exist, that is all.

Activation

I live in my present so that I can look to the future, my future is planned so that I Can live in my rarest moments.

Scripture

Galatians 2:20 I have been crucified with Christ; it is no longer I who live, but Christ lives in me; and the life which I now live in the flesh I live By faith in the Son of God, who loved me and gave Himself for me

Minister Kesha Lee

Kesha Lee is a wife, mother and grandmother, and an Automotive Technician by trade. She is the Founder of FOXXY GIRL LLC, a daughter of Zion, Prayer Warrior, Deaconess and Co-founder of God's Point of View Prayer Call.

Quote

I am an original me, who God created me to be.

I am bold yet humbled, I am different, yes very unique.

I am fearless, also faithful, my heart is forever grateful.

I am stable yet I'm mobile, I am headed international and always intentional.

Activation

Activation: I am a walking reflection of every blessing attached and appointed to my life daily, I then pour out with purpose on everyone I encounter.

Scripture

Ephesians 2:10 For we are his workmanship, created in Christ Jesus unto good works, which God hath before ordained that we should walk in them.

Lady Chanda Augustine

Bio Born on the beautiful island of Dominica is Mrs. Chanda Augustine. A woman of one husband Pastor Jefferson Augustine and mother of thee (3) children. A woman of God who stands for holiness and righteousness, she loves God and people. She is a great praise and worship leader and youth leader.

Quote

"I'm going to be me. I know who I am, I am strong,
I will determine my goals and my dreams.
I will live a life full of possibilities and fulfilment."

Activation

Because I am strong, I will live a life of possibilities.

Scripture

Ephesians 3:20 Now all glory to God, who is able through
his mighty power at work within us, to accomplish
infinitely more than we might ask or think.

Kimberly B. Curls-Feagin

Bio

Kimberly is a Wife and Mother, Woman of God and a Businesswoman. She leads her life with a servant's heart and is a game changer in every space she occupies.

"ENTHUSIASM IS THE FORCE THAT

CREATES MOMENTUM."

This quote affirms that favor and prosperity reside through the works of my hands and the results bring life and energy everywhere I go.

Give her of the the fruit of her hands, and let her works praise her in the gates.

Proverbs 31:31 — ESV

Ve-Anna S.R. Thomas

Bio

A multi-gifted individual whose motto is "Bloom Where You Are Planted." She exists to advance God's kingdom and as the founder of Ve-Anna Thomas Ministries, she develops resources to equip persons.

Life's circumstances can distract and detour you from your purpose but keep your focus, embrace every obstacle and bloom where you are planted.

Activation #1 - I am strong, I am courageous, and I can do all things because I am created in God's own image.

Activation #2 - Because of life's circumstances, I know who I am, I will walk in my calling and I will fulfill my purpose.

Activation #3 - I will bloom wherever I am planted in life.

Deuteronomy 31:6 (NIV)
Be strong and courageous. Do not be afraid or terrified because of them, for the Lord your God goes with you; he will never leave you nor forsake you.

Philippians 4:13 (NIV)
I can do all this through Him who gives me strength.

Daniel 11:32(b) (KJV)

Nona Kay Slack is a woman of purpose and business owner of Beautiful Cleaning. She is a prayer warrior and feeding the homeless in her natural calling. Nona is a mother, grandmother and great-grandmother and in all things she puts God first.

Quote

Follow your dreams.

Activation

When you follow your dreams, God will always direct
and order your steps to bring them to pass.

Scripture

Jeremiah 29: 11 For I know the plans that I have for your
declares the Lord, plans to prosper you and not to harm
you, plans to give you a hope and a future

Dr. Connie E. George

Dr Connie E. George is a born-again believer, licensed Minister of the gospel, wife, and mother. She is the current president of the Aglow International, BVI Chapter, founder of a nightly online prayer room, Prayer Warrior, Intercessor and teacher of the Word of God. Dr Connie George is an educator by profession and is currently the Chief Education Officer in British Virgin Islands. To God be the Glory!!!

Success is determination manifesting openly

Success is the result of hard work, sometimes blood, sweat, and even tears; the accomplishing dreams and aspirations.

I live for success. In Christ I have success. Every day I declare success over my life and the lives of my family because I believe that success is one of the many things that God will add to my life I manifest success daily.

Matthew 6:33 But seek ye first the kingdom of God, and his righteousness; and all these things shall be added unto you.

Lisa Arose is from St. Thomas, U.S. Virgin Islands via St. Kitts and Nevis. She is a Data Specialist and Content Creator who loves exalting the Name of the Lord.

"I Will Not Hold Myself Back. I Will Be All My Beautiful Self."

To arise and shine is a direct command from the Lord, as the "implied" subject" is "YOU". (You) arise, (you) shine! Your light **has** come, God is waiting on us to radiate His glory by living in complete obedience. It's time to be...in the present, in real time...everything that He has called us to be

Isaiah 60:1 Arise, shine, for your light has come and the glory of the Lord is risen upon you. (ESV)

Lakeysha Mattis

Lakeysha Mattis is a Master Teacher of 18 years with a passion for research, speaking, writing, and learning! She is an influencer in the areas of developing an abundant mindset, harnessing grit & building up knowledge of financial wealth pathways. Her resiliency is in learning how to rise from the ashes to greater heights despite all odds she faced throughout her life.

Quote

"If we command our wealth, we shall be rich and free. If our wealth commands us, we are poor indeed." - Edmund Burke

Activation

I decree that I am a one-percenter! I rise, thrive, and succeed in everything I set my hands to perform. Prosperity is my birthright, and I am a good manager of the resources given to me. I remember Yahweh in all I do, for He gives me the power to get wealth. Adonai gives me treasure in my sacks. I trust in Yahweh's ability to fulfill His covenant, and I am confident He looks after His word to complete it. Yahweh's gift to me is that He gives me riches and wealth to eat from and to receive my reward as I rejoice in my labor. Yahweh grants me prosperity, wealth, and honor so that my soul lacks nothing, and I declare and decree a generational wealth transfer to my future lineage.

Scripture

Proverbs 10:22 The blessing of Yahweh—it makes rich,
And He adds no grief with it.

Apostle Ava Baird

Bio — Apostle Ava Baird—Founder of Kingdom Ambassadors International House of Worship. A Women of Excellence, Motivational Speaker, Philanthropist, Entrepreneur and Author. Delights in Women's Ministry. Jesus Christ is my Everything.

Quote

There is a difference between going further and going higher; Going further is doing more of the same thing while going higher is taking it to the next level.

The brightness of your light is determined by the level of your oil!

Activation

Through my relationship with God, I seek to go higher in Him daily so that my light will illuminate the atmosphere and pierce the darkness, setting captives free.

Scripture

Isaiah 60:1 Arise, shine; for your light has come! And the glory of the Lord is risen upon thee.

Leonora Birmingham

Bio My name is Leonora Durand born on the beautiful island of Dominica residing in St. Thomas, USVI. I gave my heart to the Lord in 2022 and it was the best decision I have ever made.

Quote

"No mountain is too high to climb with God as my strength."

Activation

I am beautiful. I am unique. I am God's original design. Therefore, I am going to make a difference and stand out.

Scripture

Psalm 139:14 I will praise thee: for I am fearfully and wonderfully made: marvelous are thy works and that my soul knoweth right well.

Lady Clavia Colaire

Bio

Clavia Colaire was born on the beautiful island of Dominica, she migrated to the Virgin Islands at the age of twenty one. She was employed with Kinney Shoes where she met her husband Pastor Mcdonald Colaire. They have two beautiful young adults and presently serves at Living Word Family Ministries Church. They have owned their business Cornerstone Printing for 25years. Her heart's desire is the serve her Lord until he calls her home.

Quote

I am one of a kind, uniquely crafted by Gods loving hands.

I am still being fashioned and I'm grateful for it a gentle reminder that He is not done with me yet.

I'm at peace. I stand on Gods promises. He is with me always.

Activation

I strive for deeper depth and higher heights in Christ for that's my ultimate goal. I strive to face every day with a grateful heart and find a reason to smile.

Scripture

Psalm 127:1 Except the Lord build the house, they labour in vain that build it: except the Lord build the city, the watchman waketh but in vain.

Tiffany Lauderdale

Bio Tiffany Perise Lauderdale is a chosen woman of
GOD. She is an evangelist, psalmist, minister, sister.,
mother to K'Lon Taj, KINGdomprenuer, manager, author and visionary of LipZTalK LLC.

Quote

With GOD there is VICTORY in EVERY season and in EVERY season GOD will cause EVERYTHING to work out for your good.

Activation

I have the VICTORY In EVERY season of my life and with GOD EVERYTHING is working for my good.

Scripture

Ecclesiastes 3:1 To every thing there is a season, and a time to every purpose under the heaven.

Romans 8:28 And we know that all things work together for good to them that love God, to them who are the called according to his purpose.

Eurina Turnbull Simon was born on Tortola BVI the last daughter of her parents. At the early age of 13 she gives her heart to the Lord at a camp meeting service. Her journey in her spiritual walk became a life of prayer as she made a commitment to serve Him for the rest of her life.

Quote

"The spirit in me troubles the one in you."

Activation

Operate in the power of the Holy Spirit which is in you according to the promises given by him that lives in you.

Scripture

I John 4:4 Greater is he who is in me than he who is in the world.

Catherine Valera Fant

Catherine Fant is the C.E.O. of Gods greatest gift, Charity/Love. She strives to please God, while showing others he has no respective person. An Entrepreneur who Invented Valera's Bedding Sheet Sets.

Quote

I am encouraged! I will continue to step up and say yes to the inner spirit God is exalting within me.

Activation

Activation: #1 I am a winner, and I shall see my goals be accomplished.

Activation: #2 I am awesome and equipped to conquer all.

Scripture

Philippians 4: 13 I can do all things through Christ which strengthened me.

Ephesians 3:16 That he would grant you, according to the riches of his glory, to be strengthened with might by his spirit in the inner man.